CW01431905

ESSENTıᴀʟ

TAVIRA

TOURIST GUIDE

2024-2025

By

CARL E. FRANCIS

Table of Contents

Chapter 1

Introduction to Tavira: Essential Details to know

Tavira, a hidden treasure in Portugal's eastern Algarve area, is tucked away along the Gilão River and is renowned for its historical importance, distinct character, and stunning scenery. This town is a captivating location for tourists looking for a combination of culture, leisure, and adventure since it skillfully combines the old past with contemporary energy.

Culture and history

The Phoenicians, Romans, Moors, and even the Knights of Santiago left their mark on Tavira's more than 2,000-year history. The town's architecture, in particular, reflects this rich historical tapestry. From the imposing Igreja de Santa Maria do Castelo, where knights of the Order of Santiago are interred, to the Roman bridge (which, strangely, was reconstructed during the Renaissance), a walk around Tavira displays relics from several historical periods. The town's 37 churches, including the Renaissance masterpiece Igreja da Misericórdia, bear witness to its enduring religious and cultural significance.

Tavira offers a laid-back lifestyle that combines traditional customs with modern conveniences, despite its rich historical background. Encircling Tavira with a network of lagoons and barrier islands, the Ria Formosa Natural Park is a sanctuary for nature lovers and birdwatchers, providing some of the Algarve's most stunning beaches. Local festivals, where customs like Fado music—Portugal's soulful folk genre—reverberate through the streets, further showcase Tavira's cultural pulse.

20 Interesting Tavira Facts

Here are some entertaining and fascinating facts about Tavira to add to the enjoyment of your visit:

- Roman Bridge, Not So Roman: Tavira's well-known bridge was reconstructed during the Renaissance, which is why it was given the name "Roman."
- One of the smallest rivers: The Séqua River is one of the smallest rivers in the world, having changed its name from the Gilão River under the Roman bridge.
- Tavira has 37 churches, making it one of the cities in Portugal with the greatest "church-to-people" ratios.
- The finest salt: Some of the world's finest salt is produced at Tavira's salt pans.

- One of Europe's most significant wetlands, the Ria Formosa, is home to flamingos and other migrating birds. Tavira is a portion of this bird paradise.
- Known for Tuna: Tavira has a long history of fishing for tuna, and some of Portugal's finest tinned tuna can still be found here.
- The Hidden Paradise of Ilha de Tavira: Tavira's island beach is regarded as one of the greatest, although it is still very uncrowded.
- A Castle with a Garden View: Tavira's Moorish-era castle provides a breathtaking vista of the town's gardens and roofs.
- Fishing Festival Fun: Tavira celebrates its seaside roots with yearly fishing festivals that include seafood feasts.
- Cork is King: Tavira is close to Portugal's cork-producing areas, and local stores sell a wide variety of cork items.
- Roman remains beneath the town: Tavira has been connected to ancient Roman cities by archaeologists who have found Roman remains beneath portions of the town.
- Algarve Octopus Capital: The neighboring town of Santa Luzia, which is a part of the municipality of Tavira, is well-known for being the Algarve's octopus capital.

- Portugal's "Tile Town": Tavira's buildings have some of the most exquisitely maintained azulejos, or ceramic tiles.
- Portuguese Phoenician Links: Tavira's old nautical culture was influenced by the Phoenician colony, which dates back to around 1000 B.C.
- Fish Can't Swim Here: According to legend, fish are confused by Tavira's Roman bridge because the river current stops flowing exactly underneath it.
- Ghost Stories from the Old Town: People in Tavira's old town, especially near its historic churches, rumor of ghost sightings.
- Home of the Oldest Olive Trees: The landscape around Tavira is home to some of Portugal's oldest olive trees.
- Historical Sweets: Tavira's pastries, such as the "Queijo de Figo," are made using recipes that have been handed down through the ages.
- A Roofless Church: Due to 18th-century earthquake damage, Tavira possesses a destroyed church without a roof.
- The Mysterious Tavira Bell: When rung at midnight, one of Tavira's bells, which is kept in the Church of Santa Maria, is said to possess magical abilities.

Other Things Travelers Must Have

A camera is a must while visiting Tavira because of the breathtaking surroundings, but don't forget useful things like sunscreen, particularly if you want to explore the beaches or take leisurely walks along the river. History enthusiasts, foodies (particularly those who like seafood), and casual walkers will all enjoy Tavira. The remainder of the Algarve, which is renowned for its varied scenery and quaint seaside villages, is also a great place to start your exploration.

This town provides a peaceful getaway in nature as well as a cultural trip through history, whether you want to explore its cobblestone streets or unwind on Ilha de Tavira.

Tavira's topography, climate, and population

The charming town of Tavira, located in Portugal's Algarve, is renowned for its beautiful scenery and rich cultural legacy. Because of its position on the southeast coast, the town has a distinct mix of Atlantic and Mediterranean influences that have shaped its terrain, demographic trends, and weather patterns. This section offers a thorough examination of Tavira's topography, climate, weather patterns, and inhabitants.

Tavira's topography

Tavira's terrain combines undulating hills, coastal plains, and the distinctive lagoon system of the Ria Formosa Natural Park in a harmonic way.

Beaches and Coastal Areas: Tavira is located on the shore, which has some of the Algarve's most stunning beaches. Long expanses of sandy beaches and placid seas may be found along the somewhat flat coastline. One of the town's most well-known beaches is Ilha de Tavira, a barrier island with immaculate white sand and crystal-clear seas that are ideal for swimming and tanning.

One of the most significant wetlands in Europe is the vast lagoon system known as Ria Formosa, which is situated off the coast of Tavira. Salt marshes, mudflats, and tidal canals make up the Ria Formosa, which is an essential habitat for marine life and migrating birds.

Agriculture and Inland Hills: The landscape changes as you go inland, displaying gently undulating hills and valleys. Agriculture makes up the majority of the land in these locations, especially the production of carob trees, citrus fruits, and olives. Small, traditional villages dot the interior regions as well, providing a window into the Algarve's rustic way of life.

Tavira's climate

Tavira has hot, dry summers and warm, wet winters due to its Mediterranean climate (Köppen-Geiger Csa).

Although Tavira's closeness to the Atlantic Ocean tempers some of the intense heat experienced further inland, this climatic type is characteristic of most of the southern Iberian Peninsula.

Average Annual Temperature: July and August are the hottest months, with average temperatures ranging from 26°C to 30°C (79°F to 86°F). The average annual temperature in Tavira is around 18°C (64°F). The average temperature during the mild winter months is between 11°C and 17°C (52°F and 63°F).

Rainfall Patterns: December and January are the wettest months in Tavira, with the majority of rainfall occurring between November and February. The town is one of the driest areas in Portugal, with an average of 500 mm (19.7 inches) of rain falling there each year. Because there is hardly little rain throughout the summer, the area experiences dry, arid conditions.

Sunlight Hours: With more than 3,000 hours of sunlight annually, Tavira is renowned for its abundance of sunshine. This makes it the perfect place for anyone looking to take a vacation in the sun and escape colder areas. The sunniest months are June through September when there are sunny days and a clear sky.

Tavira's population

Although there are around 26,000 people living in Tavira, this number varies greatly throughout the busiest travel season. Compared to other Algarve cities, Tavira has a lower population density, which makes it a more peaceful and laid-back place to visit.

Tavira's population is mostly Portuguese, although there are also an increasing number of foreigners living there, especially Northern European seniors. The foreign population in Tavira is mostly composed of expatriates from the United Kingdom, Germany, and the Netherlands. The town's pleasant temperature, reasonable cost of living, and tranquil environment attract a lot of these foreigners.

Impact of Tourism: Tavira's population may increase during the summer as visitors from all over Europe swarm to its beaches and historical landmarks. Many companies in the hospitality and service sectors depend on the annual flood of tourists, which is why tourism is vital to the local economy.

Cultural Influences: The Moors, Romans, and Phoenicians left their mark on Tavira's architecture, food, and customs, and the town's rich historical legacy is reflected in its populace. Additionally, the town is renowned for its strong sense of community, which is fostered via local celebrations and festivals.

Local Economy and Employment: Tavira's economy is based mostly on tourism, fishing, and agriculture. Citrus fruits, olives, and almonds are grown in the Algarve's lush soils, and fishing, especially for shellfish, is still a major source of income on the Ria Formosa. With so many residents working in hotels, restaurants, and other tourist-related establishments, tourism has grown in importance in recent years.

Language and Currency

Language:

Tavira, like the rest of Portugal, speaks Portuguese as its official language. Portuguese, the sixth most spoken language in the world, is a Romance language that is related to Spanish, Italian, and French. English is generally understood in Tavira, even though the majority of the locals speak Portuguese, particularly in tourism-oriented establishments like hotels, restaurants, and stores. Due to the large number of international tourists, especially from the UK, Germany, and other European countries, many people who work in the hospitality sector speak English well. Nonetheless, knowing a few simple Portuguese words may improve your trip and is often valued by locals.

Currency:

Tavira and Portugal both utilize the Euro (€) as their official currency. The standard currency throughout the majority of the European Union is the euro, which is split into 100 cents. In addition to 1 and 2 euros, coins come in values of 1, 2, 5, 10, 20, and 50 cents. The denominations of banknotes include 5, 10, 20, 50, 100, 200, and 500 euros; however, the 200 and 500 euro notes are not as often used.

Currency Exchange: Tavira offers a comprehensive range of currency exchange services. Banks, currency exchange offices, or automated teller machines (known locally as multibancos) are the places where visitors may exchange their money. There are several ATMs in the town, and the majority of them accept debit and credit cards from other countries. To prevent any problems with using cards overseas, it's a beneficial idea to let your bank know about your trip schedule.

Credit and Debit Cards: Most businesses, particularly those in tourist regions, take credit and debit cards. However, it is advised to have some cash on hand for smaller purchases, such as those made at local markets, cafés, or in rural locations.

Tipping Culture: Although not required, tipping is welcomed in Tavira. Depending on the level of service, it is typical to tip between 5 and 10% of the entire cost while dining at a restaurant. Small gratuities may also be given to hotel employees and taxi drivers, although this is up to the individual.

Travelers may more easily tour Tavira and take advantage of the town's rich culture and friendliness by being familiar with the fundamentals of the local language and money.

Chapter 2
How to Plan a Successful Vacation to Tavira

To guarantee a seamless and delightful journey, careful planning is necessary when planning a vacation to Tavira or any other location. A well-planned schedule is essential to getting the most out of your trip, from selecting the ideal travel dates to packing sensibly, thinking about lodging, and organizing your activities. Here is a thorough resource to help travelers plan a successful trip:

1. Choose a time to go to Tavira.

Tavira is a year-round resort due to its Mediterranean environment, which has scorching summers and pleasant winters. However, the activities you choose to prioritize will determine the ideal time to visit:

One of the nicest seasons to go is in the spring (March-May). The pleasant weather, blossoming flowers, and lush vegetation make it ideal for outdoor pursuits like hiking, strolling, and seeing Tavira's historical sites. Accommodation costs are often cheaper than at the busiest time of year, and crowds are less.

Summer (June to September): This is the best season if you like the beach. Enjoying Tavira's breathtaking beaches, including Ilha de Tavira, is made possible by the hot, sunny weather. But because this is the busiest travel time of year, anticipate more people and more expensive lodging. If you want to travel in the summer, it is advised that you make reservations in advance.

Autumn (October to November): This is a terrific time of year for a more laid-back and economical trip since the weather is still lovely and the beaches are less crowded. Opportunities for outdoor activities are also available throughout this season, particularly if you like to explore Tavira's natural settings.

Winter (December to February): Compared to northern Europe, winter provides a favorable environment, albeit being wetter and colder than other seasons. It's a wonderful time to explore local culture, travel to historical landmarks, and take in the town without the summer crowds.

2. Make reservations for lodging in advance.

Tavira has a range of lodging choices, from opulent hotels to comfortable guesthouses and affordable hostels. You have a higher chance of getting your desired accommodation the sooner you make your reservation, particularly if you're going during the busiest summer months.

Numerous hotels and resorts can be found in Tavira, some of which have views of the Ria Formosa lagoon or access to the beach. Seek lodging that has received positive evaluations, ideally near the attractions or beaches you want to see.

Bed & Breakfasts (B&Bs) and guesthouses: If you want a more genuine experience, think about booking a room in a nearby B&B or guesthouse. These smaller businesses often provide individualized care and a cozy setting.

Vacation Rentals and Apartments: Hiring a vacation villa or apartment is a common choice, particularly for families or groups. There are other possibilities available on websites like Airbnb, which let you stay in more residential locations and get a closer look at the local way of life.

3. Research and arrange activities

Tavira is well-known for its breathtaking beaches, historical sites, and closeness to natural areas. To make the most of your vacation, start researching the best sights and things to do before your trip. Here are some ideas:

Exploration of History and Culture: Tavira has a rich past, and sites like the Roman Bridge, Igreja do Misericórdia, and the Tavira Castle provide insight into the town's past. Make time to explore the old town's quaint streets and schedule trips to these locations during the cooler hours of the day.

Outdoor Activities: Nature enthusiasts will find paradise in the neighboring Ria Formosa Natural Park. You may explore the lagoon and its varied species by hiking, biking, birding, or taking a boat excursion. A must-see location for swimming, water sports, and sunbathing is Tavira's Ilha de Tavira beach.

Day excursions: Take into account organizing day excursions to neighboring towns like Olhão or Faro. Since the Algarve is a small area, Tavira is easily accessible by car from a number of locations.

Local Markets & Food Tours: Tavira's local markets, such as the Mercado da Ribeira, provide an opportunity to sample Portuguese food and purchase fresh seafood, vegetables, and handicrafts. Furthermore, cooking workshops or food tours may provide a more in-depth exploration of the local cuisine, particularly with regard to seafood.

4. Make a Transportation Plan

If you prepare beforehand, learning about Tavira and the Algarve area may be simple. Here are some transportation options:

Air Travel: Faro Airport, the closest airport, is around 40 minutes' drive from Tavira. This is a wonderful place to start your adventure since it's where many foreign aircraft arrive. Tavira may be reached from Faro by taxi, shuttle bus, or rental vehicle.

Public Transportation: Tavira is connected to other Algarve cities by a dependable rail and bus system. For shorter journeys near Tavira, buses are an alternative, but trains are a fantastic way to see the Algarve coastline. Trains operated by CP (Comboios de Portugal) commonly travel between Tavira and Faro.

Car Rental: If you want the freedom to go outside of Tavira at your own speed, renting a car is a wonderful choice. The Algarve's roads are usually in excellent shape, and hiring a vehicle makes it simple to go to far-flung beaches and interior sights.

Walking and Bicycles: Tavira is a relatively walkable town, and many visitors choose to explore it on foot, particularly to the ancient town and the neighboring beaches. An excellent method to get more mileage while still taking in the beautiful scenery is to hire a bike.

5. Get important documents ready.

Make sure you have the required paperwork and information on hand before you leave.

Passport and Visa Requirements: For visits of up to 90 days, the majority of visitors from the EU, USA, and Canada do not need a visa. However, make sure your passport is valid for the length of your trip and always verify the particular criteria of your nation.

Travel Insurance: Getting travel insurance before your journey is strongly advised. Medical costs, travel cancellations, lost baggage, and other unanticipated events that may occur during your vacation should all be covered by descent insurance.

Health Precautions: Although Portugal is a safe nation, it's a sensible idea to pack sunscreen, basic medicines, and any prescription drugs you may have. Although there are no particular immunizations needed to enter the nation, it is advisable to review health precautions before departing.

6. Pack wisely.

Making the right travel packing choices may have a significant impact. For most of the year, Tavira's mild Mediterranean environment necessitates wearing light, breathable clothes, but it's also vital to take the time of year into account.

7. Keep yourself informed and safe.

It's important to keep up with any local laws or travel warnings that can impact your trip. Even though Tavira is a typically extremely secure town, it's wise to travel with common sense.

Emergency Numbers: If you have a police, fire, or medical emergency, you may call Portugal's emergency number, 112.

Travel Updates: If you depend on public transit, be sure to keep up with any changes to the timetable or local news.

You may make sure your vacation to Tavira is well-planned and successful by following these tips. Planning beforehand can help you make the most of this lovely town and its environs, whether you're here for a leisurely beach holiday or a cultural adventure.

Chapter 3
Ideal Seasons Tourists Should Visit Tavira

Tavira's Mediterranean climate makes it a year-round destination in Portugal's Algarve area. However, factors like weather, activity, and population density all influence the "ideal" time of year for travelers. Every season in Tavira offers special advantages and charms for tourists. Let's examine the ideal times to visit Tavira in light of the many seasons, their characteristics, and the advantages they provide for various kinds of travelers.

Spring: March to May

One of the best seasons to visit Tavira is in the spring when temperatures range from 15°C (59°F) to 25°C (77°F). With flowers in bloom, verdant scenery, and a bright sky, the Algarve's natural splendor is at its peak at this time of year. Tavira is ideal for outdoor sports and sightseeing because of its pleasant, warm climate, which includes milder mornings and nights.

Advantages for Travelers:

Outdoor Exploration: Without the extreme heat of summer, spring is a wonderful time to see the town's historic landmarks, like the Roman Bridge, the Tavira Castle, and the quaint old town's cobblestone streets.

Perfect Weather for Hiking and Birdwatching: Springtime brings life to the Ria Formosa Natural Park in Tavira. Both local birds, like flamingos, and migratory species are visible to birdwatchers. Hiking and cycling in the natural reserves, salt pans, and other rural regions are also made possible by the pleasant weather.

Fewer Crowds: Compared to the summer, spring will be less crowded since it is still regarded as the shoulder season. This makes it possible to enjoy the town in a more laid-back, genuine way without the rush.

Reduced Costs: Spring is a more affordable time of year since lodging and airfare are often less expensive. Off-season discounts are available to visitors, particularly in April and May.

Summer: June to September

Tavira's summer months, when temperatures climb between 25°C (77°F) and 35°C (95°F), are the busiest travel seasons. It is a popular spot for beachgoers and sunseekers because of the long, hot days and plenty of sunlight. During the summer, Tavira's beaches—including Ilha de Tavira—become popular destinations.

Advantages for Travelers:

Beach Fun: The finest season for beachgoers is summer. The long sandy island of Ilha de Tavira, which is reachable by boat, is ideal for swimming, sunbathing, and water activities like paddle boarding and windsurfing. Swimming is especially pleasant because of the mild water temperatures.

Bright Ambience: Summer festivals, outdoor marketplaces, and cultural events bring Tavira to life. Bars and restaurants are open late into the night, and the nightlife is lively. While taking in the celebratory environment, visitors may savor the native Portuguese cuisine, which includes fresh seafood.

Extended Daylight: Travelers may fit more activities into their days because of the longer days. Tourists may participate in beach activities in the afternoon, go sightseeing in the morning, and eat al fresco at sunset.

Ideal for Families: Because of the school vacations, summer is often preferred by families. With shallow beaches and plenty of kid-friendly activities like boat cruises and island visits, Tavira is a wonderful place for families.

Summer's drawbacks

Crowds and High Prices: Larger crowds are a result of the busiest travel season, particularly at well-known beaches and attractions. Booking far in advance is advised to ensure accommodations during this season since hotel and rental rates are at their highest.

Extreme Heat: The summer heat may be unbearable for some people, especially while they are touring. Wearing sunscreen and staying hydrated are crucial while traveling at this time of year.

Autumn: October to November

Tavira's climate is more temperate in the fall, with highs of 17°C (63°F) to 25°C (77°F). After the summer rush, the people start to thin out, but the weather is still nice, so this is another excellent time to go if you want a more laid-back, peaceful getaway.

Advantages for Travelers:

Milder Weather: Cooler, more agreeable temperatures replace the scorching summer heat. Because of this, fall is the ideal season for sightseeing, walking tours, and sweat-free exploration of Tavira's historical and cultural landmarks.

Enjoying the Beaches Without Crowds: In October, especially, the beaches are still nice for swimming and tanning even as the water cools. Tourists may enjoy more space and peace since there aren't as many people throughout the summer.

Festivals and Local Markets: In the fall, Tavira's local markets, such as the Mercado da Ribeira, are still bustling. Enjoy culinary festivals that honor the harvest season and take in the fresh products of the area.

Reduced Costs: As fewer people travel, the cost of lodging and airfare tends to go down as well. Autumn travel is more cost-effective, particularly in November when off-season savings are available.

Winter: December to February

Compared to northern Europe, Tavira has moderate winters with temperatures between 10°C (50°F) and 17°C (63°F). Even though it's the wettest season, Tavira receives very little precipitation in comparison to other regions of Portugal, and many days are still sunny and bright.

Advantages for Travelers:

Calm and Quiet: Tavira is most peaceful in the winter. This is the perfect time of year if you want to get away from the crowd and have a quiet getaway. The town slows down, allowing visitors to enjoy real local life.

Cultural Exploration: Tavira's museums, galleries, and cathedrals are best visited in the winter. Less crowded locations that provide a more personal glimpse of the town's cultural legacy are the Igreja da Misericórdia and Palácio da Galeria.

Budget-Friendly Travel: Because airfare and lodging are at their lowest, now is the most economical time to go. Budget-conscious tourists may still enjoy Tavira's beauty while taking advantage of winter savings.

Christmas and New Year: Tavira's streets are illuminated for the holidays, adding to the season's festive enchantment. During this time of year, the town offers a distinctive cultural experience via tiny local activities.

Winter's drawbacks

Cooler Weather: Although the temperature is lower than in other parts of Europe, it may still be too cold for some beach activities. Warm clothing is a must for visitors, particularly at night.

Limited Activities: There could not be access to some seasonal activities, especially those involving the beach and water sports. Still, this time of year is ideal for learning about culture and history.

General Crucial Advice for Tavira Travel in Any Season

No matter the season, there are a few key pointers that can ensure your journey to Tavira goes smoothly:

1. For the busiest times, make reservations in advance.

Make sure to reserve your lodging and airfare well in advance if you want to go to Tavira during the summer. Prices often soar as the day draws near, and hotels and resorts fill up fast. Making a reservation in advance guarantees the best rates and your desired accommodation.

2. Pack seasonally

Spring and fall: Wearing layers is essential since the noontime temperatures are milder and the mornings and nights may be chilly. Remember to wear comfortable walking shoes.

Summer: Sunglasses, sunscreen, a hat, and light, breathable clothes are necessities. It's also crucial to include a reusable water bottle since Tavira may become really hot.

Winter: Pack warm clothes for the likelihood of rain and chilly evenings, even when the weather is nice. For most days, a lightweight sweater or jacket will do.

3. Think about hiring a car rental.

Renting a vehicle is an excellent choice if you want to see more of the Algarve. Tavira is near a number of other quaint villages, and you may go at your own speed if you have your own car.

4. Examine the festivals and events in your area.

From music festivals in the summer to harvest festivities in the fall, Tavira organizes several events all year long. Before you go, determine if there are any festivals you can attend by looking at the local event calendar.

5. Pay attention to the Siesta Hours.

Due to the Portuguese custom of siesta, a lot of stores and establishments shut in the afternoon, often from 1 to 3 p.m. To minimize any disruption, schedule your errands or shopping around this break.

6. Make use of public transit.

Tavira offers excellent public transportation alternatives, such as buses and trains that link the town to other areas of the Algarve if you don't intend to hire a vehicle. For regional travel, the Comboios de Portugal (CP) rail service is effective.

Items to Bring on the Trip

Whether you're going on a lengthy vacation or just a quick weekend trip, packing might be a little difficult. In addition to keeping your baggage small and manageable, knowing what to pack is essential to making sure you're ready for everything.

1. Travel Essentials and Documents

Make sure that all of your trip paperwork and other goods are securely packed before considering clothes or electronics. These are the most important items to carry because losing them could ruin your trip.

Crucial Documents:

Passport/ID Card: The most important thing to have while going abroad is your passport. Make sure it remains valid for a minimum of six months after the dates of your trip. Bring an ID card or any other necessary form of identification if you are going domestically.

Visas: You may need to get a visa ahead of time, depending on where you're going. Keep printed e-visas and other documentation with your passport.

Boarding Pass: Verify that you have access to your boarding pass or check-in details, whether it is printed or on your phone.

Travel Insurance: Always bring emergency contact information and a copy of your travel insurance policy.

Vacation Itinerary: It's helpful to have a copy of your vacation itinerary on hand, complete with airline numbers, hotel, and transportation arrangements.

Credit/Debit Cards: In the event that one of your payment methods fails or is misplaced, always have two on hand. If you are going abroad, let your bank know to prevent any problems using your card.

Local Currency: When you arrive at your location, have some cash on hand for little costs like snacks or taxi fare.

Driver's License/International Driving Permit: Bring your driver's license and, if required, an international driving permit if you want to hire a vehicle.

Vaccination/Health Documentation: Bring any relevant health documentation or vaccination certificates needed for admission into certain countries as a result of new travel requirements brought on by the COVID-19 epidemic and other health issues.

2. Packing equipment and luggage

Selecting the appropriate baggage is essential for a hassle-free journey. The kind of trip will determine whether you choose a suitcase, backpack, or duffel bag, but always take portability, size, and durability into account.

Luggage Essentials:

Suitcase or Travel Bag: It's important to have a roomy, sturdy, and lightweight suitcase or travel bag. For convenient movement, think about one with wheels or backpack straps.

Packing Cubes: Keep everything tidy and small by using these practical cubes to arrange your clothes. For clothing, accessories, and toiletries, use various sizes.

A daypack or tote bag is a smaller bag that may be used for excursions or day trips, or it can be used to carry necessities like food, water bottles, and travel guides.

Bring TSA-approved locks for your baggage for extra protection, particularly if you're traveling with checked luggage.

Reusable Tote Bags: These lightweight bags are useful for packing light and for shopping or transporting additional stuff on the move.

Luggage Tags: Ensure that your name and contact details are prominently displayed on the luggage tag of your backpack or suitcase.

3. Clothes and shoes.

It might be challenging to pack enough clothing for your vacation without going overboard. Here are some tips for packing sensibly for various hobbies and climates.

General Advice on Clothing:

Layering Pieces: Pack adaptable layering pieces, such as light jackets, cardigans, or scarves, depending on the environment where you're going. As the temperature changes, they are simple to add or remove.

Comfortable Shoes: Bring breathable, comfortable shoes, such as walking sandals or sneakers, for strolling or touring. Bring dress shoes or chic flats if you're going to a formal function or dining out.

Lightweight Travel Clothes: Choose clothing composed of materials that are resistant to wrinkles and lightweight. Bring neutral hues that you can mix and combine to get a variety of looks.

Outerwear: Bring a down jacket that is simple to compress or a lightweight, warm jacket if you're going somewhere chilly.

Rain Gear: It's essential to have a tiny umbrella or packable rain jacket, particularly if you're going somewhere with erratic weather.

Formal or Specialty Clothing: Bring suitable clothing, such as a lovely dress, swimwear, or hiking gear, if you want to attend formal events, eat at fancy restaurants, or engage in certain sports (such as swimming or trekking).

Clothing for Various Climates:

Warm Climates: Your packing list should be dominated by swimwear, breathable dresses, shorts, t-shirts, and lightweight apparel. Remember to wear a wide-brimmed hat and sunglasses to protect yourself from the sun.

In colder climates, pack a thick scarf, beanies, gloves, and thermal layers. Select layers of clothes, such as sweaters, thick socks, and long-sleeved shirts, to stay warm.

In wet or rainy climates, bring a rain jacket, waterproof shoes, and quick-dry clothing.

4. Personal Care and Toiletries

Travel-sized goods or multipurpose items might save space since personal care and toiletries can be heavy.

Essential Personal Care Items:

Travel-size toothbrushes and toothpaste are ideal for conserving space.

Choose travel-sized bottles or solid bars for your shampoo and conditioner. As an alternative, a lot of hotels provide these.

Body wash or soap: Pack a travel-sized body wash or a little bar of soap.

Razor and Shaving Cream: A little razor kit or disposable razors are helpful.

Deodorant: An essential item for every journey.

Skincare Products: Bring along your everyday necessities, such as lip balm, sunscreen, and moisturizer. Don't bring full bottles; travel-sized ones will work just fine.

Makeup Kit: For those who use makeup, a compact cosmetic kit including multipurpose items such as mascara, BB cream, and multipurpose lipstick will help you maintain a more efficient beauty regimen.

Hairbrush/comb and Hair Ties: Travel-friendly, small brushes are ideal, as are any required hair ties or clips.

Prescription Drugs: Pack adequate prescription drugs for the duration of your vacation, as well as any relevant medical records.

First Aid Kit: It is always helpful to have a modest, travel-sized first-aid kit containing bandages, disinfectant wipes, and painkillers.

5. Electronics and Devices

Electronics and gadgets are essential to contemporary travel since they let you remain in touch, take pictures, and easily explore new locations.

Smartphone and Charger: With its dual functions as a camera, GPS, and entertainment device, your smartphone is perhaps the most multipurpose item you'll need. Remember to include the charger and, if required, an international converter.

Power Bank: During a long day of touring, a portable power bank makes sure your phone or other gadgets don't run out of charge.

Camera: Bring a camera with additional memory cards and batteries if you like taking pictures.

Travel adaptor: Make sure you have an adaptor that is compatible with the country where you are going, particularly for charging electrical devices.

Laptop or Tablet: You may require a laptop or tablet if you need to work or want to be entertained. To minimize weight and room on shorter journeys, think about leaving items behind.

Earbuds or headphones: Perfect for lounging at your lodging and on lengthy bus or airplane rides.

Books or an e-reader: If you like reading, an e-reader is a portable method to carry a lot of books without adding bulk.

6. Unique Things for Various Journeys

There can be certain things you need to bring, depending on why you are traveling:

Beach Vacation: To safeguard your gadgets, bring a waterproof bag, flip-flops, a beach towel, sunglasses, and sunscreen.

A map or GPS, hiking boots, a reusable water bottle, and weather-appropriate clothing, such as moisture-wicking clothing, are essential for any adventure or hiking trip.

Professional Trip: Essentials include a laptop, a portable charger, and a suit or other professional clothes. Additionally, bring a small bag of toiletries so you may freshen yourself during lengthy conferences or meetings.

Cultural Destinations: To respect local traditions, bring suitable attire, such as long sleeves and slacks, if you're traveling to a religious or conservative country.

7. Health and Safety Items

Items related to health and safety have become even more important in the modern travel environment.

Face masks: Bring a few disposable or reusable masks, particularly for public transportation and airports.

Hand Sanitizer: Keeping your hands clean requires a tiny bottle of hand sanitizer, especially in locations where soap and water may not be easily accessible.

Disinfectant wipes are helpful for cleaning surfaces such as restaurant tables, door knobs, and airline trays.

A travel pillow and an eye mask may significantly improve your ability to fall asleep on lengthy flights or bus rides.

It takes great preparation and consideration to pack for a trip. You'll be ready for any kind of vacation if you divide your packing list into categories such as necessities like clothes, electronics, toiletries, and travel papers. Whether you're going on a hiking trek, city adventure, or beach vacation, packing little yet effective will guarantee a comfortable and easy journey. Be sure to adjust your packing list according to the activities you have planned, the location, and the weather.

Chapter 4
Accommodation Options for Tourists

Tavira has a diverse choice of lodging alternatives, making it an attractive location for tourists of all budgets and interests. Tavira's hotels and guest houses provide something for everyone, whether you want luxury, family-friendly, or more inexpensive accommodations. To assist you find the finest place to stay in Tavira, we've compiled a comprehensive list of the top ten hotels, complete with locations, major features, and pricing ranges.

1. Tavira Convent Guest House

- **Address:** Rua Dom Paio Peres Correia, 8800-407 Tavira.
- **Price range**: €150 to €300 per night.

The Pousada Convento de Tavira, set in a 16th-century convent, combines historical elegance with contemporary conveniences. The rooms have been carefully refurbished, keeping the historic architecture while providing luxury amenities. Guests may unwind by the outdoor pool or discover the central cloister garden. This hotel is ideal for history buffs seeking a unique and elegant stay.

Features:

- Historic architecture with a mix of contemporary conveniences
- Outdoor pool and a lovely yard
- The on-site restaurant serves regional cuisine.
- Walking distance to Tavira Castle and the Roman Bridge.

2. Vila Galé de Tavira

- **Address:** Rua 4 de Outubro, 8800-362 Tavira.
- **Price range:** €90 to €180 per night.

Vila Gale Tavira is a family-friendly hotel on the Tavira River with spacious rooms and a variety of services including a huge swimming pool, a wellness center, and a children's club. It's great for families or parties seeking a calm and convenient stay.

Features:

- Large outdoor swimming pool.
- Spa & Wellness Center
- On-site eateries and bars.
- Perfect for families and groups.

3. Hotel Rural Quinta do Marco

- **Address:** Sitio do Marco, 632A, 8800-164 Tavira.
- **Price range:** €70 to €150 per night.

Nestled in the Algarve countryside, this hotel provides a peaceful and environmentally friendly vacation. Hotel Rural Quinta do Marco is bordered by orchards and olive trees and offers magnificent views of the hills and sea. Guests may go hiking, cycling, or rest by the pool.

Features:

- Beautiful rural vistas.
- Outdoor pool and health facility.
- The on-site restaurant serves organic vegetables.
- Ideal for nature enthusiasts and environmentally conscientious visitors.

4. AP Maria Nova Lounge Hotel

- **Address:** Rua Antonio Pinheiro, 8800-323 Tavira.
- **Price range**: €80 to €160 per night.

This adults-only hotel offers a calm and sophisticated refuge for couples and lonely visitors. The hotel has contemporary, elegant décor and a rooftop pool with magnificent views of Tavira. It's an excellent option for a romantic trip.

Features:

- Rooftop pool with city views.
- Spa and Wellness Services
- Bar and restaurant serving Mediterranean food.
- Adult-only policy for a calmer environment.

5. Ozadi Tavira Hotel.

- **Address:** Quinta das Oliveiras, E. N. 125, 8800-053 Tavira.
- **Price range**: €100 to €200 per night.

The Ozadi Tavira Hotel combines modern style with historic accents to create a fashionable, friendly ambiance. This hotel has big accommodations, a huge outdoor pool, and a variety of eating choices, making it ideal for families and couples alike.

Features:

- Outdoor pool and sun patio
- Family-friendly, with a kids' club.
- Gym and Wellness Center
- On-site eateries provide both local and foreign food.

6. Quinta Do Caracol

- **Address:** Rua de São Pedro 11, 8800-405, Tavira.
- **Price range:** €90 to €140 per night.

Quinta do Caracol is a beautiful guesthouse located in a typical Algarvian home, providing a comfortable and personalized stay in Tavira. This hotel, surrounded by beautiful grounds, is excellent for visitors seeking a calm refuge near the city center.

Features:

- Beautiful garden setting.
- Outdoor pool.
- Traditional architecture and contemporary facilities.
- Walking distance from Tavira's major attractions.

7. Tavira House

- **Address:** Rua Dr. Augusto Silva Carvalho 11, 8800-324 Tavira.
- **Price range:** €100 to €180 per night.

Tavira House, located in the center of the city, provides a boutique experience inside an 18th-century house. The hotel mixes historical elements with contemporary comfort to create an intimate and sophisticated setting.

Features:

- Boutique hotel with historical charm.
- Rooftop Terrace with City Views
- Personalized service.
- Ideal for couples and visitors who want a unique experience.

8. Cabana Park Resort

- **Address:** Cabanas de Tavira, 8800-591 Tavira
- **Price range:** €70 to €120 per night.

This family-friendly resort is situated in the adjacent community of Cabanas and provides access to the stunning Ria Formosa Natural Park. The resort offers contemporary apartments with kitchenettes, ideal for extended stays or family holidays.

Features:

- Self-catering apartments include kitchenettes.
- Outdoor pools and kids' play places
- proximity to beaches and ecological parks.
- Ideal for families or extended visits.

9. Pedras del Rei

- **Price range:** €60 to €130 per night.

Pedras d'el Rei is a resort community with villas and apartments near the popular Barril Beach. This property is ideal for families or parties looking to combine the natural beauty of the Algarve with the ease of self-catering lodgings.

Features:

- Villas and flats with kitchens
- Close to Barril Beach and Ria Formosa.
- Outdoor pool and tennis courts.
- Family-friendly environment with activities for children.

10. Vila Gale Albacora.

- **Address:** Quatro Águas, 8800-901 Tavira.
- **Price range**: €90 to €180 per night.

Vila Gale Albacora, located in a restored tuna fishing community, provides a unique cultural experience. The hotel is situated in the Ria Formosa Natural Park, which provides a tranquil and attractive location. Guests may go on boat rides, nature excursions, or rest by the pool.

Features:

- Located in a historic tuna fishing community.
- Spa, Wellness Center, and Outdoor Pool
- Access to boat rides and wildlife excursions.
- Family-friendly, with cultural attractions nearby.

Tips for Selecting Accommodation in Tavira

- Consider Location: If you want to be near the town's major attractions, book lodgings in the city center or along the riverbank. Hotels in the countryside or along the Ria Formosa are suitable for a more relaxed atmosphere.
- Book Early for High Season: Tavira is a popular location, especially during the summer months, so book ahead of time if you want to visit during peak season.
- Facilities: Depending on your trip requirements, check for hotels that provide certain facilities like swimming pools, spas, or family-friendly features.
- Budget-Friendly Options: Tavira has a variety of lodgings to suit various budgets. There's something for everyone, from elegant historical hotels to budget-friendly guesthouses and apartment rentals.

Alternatives to hotels

1. Vacation rentals (Airbnb, VRBO, etc.)

Budget: €50 to €150 per night, depending on location and size.

Vacation rentals are a popular alternative to hotels, offering tourists home-like lodgings. Tavira offers a diverse variety of other options, from modest flats in the city center to bigger villas in more distant places.

Vacation rentals sometimes have fully outfitted kitchens, living areas, and, in some cases, private gardens or pools. They are great for families or parties seeking more room, privacy, and the ability to prepare their meals, which may considerably reduce daily expenditures.

Popular vacation rental areas in Tavira:

City Center Apartments: Located near Tavira's major attractions, such as the Roman Bridge and Tavira Castle, these rentals are ideal for people looking to be close to cafés, restaurants, and stores.

Rural Villas: For those seeking peace, renting a villa in the surrounding countryside or the Ria Formosa Natural Park provides an ideal refuge.

2. Hostels

Budget: €15 to €40 per night.

Hostels are a low-cost choice for solitary travelers, backpackers, and anybody searching for economical lodging. Tavira has various hostels offering both dormitory-style and individual rooms. Most hostels provide common spaces, kitchens, and sometimes scheduled excursions or social activities, making them an excellent place to meet other travelers.

Notable hostels in Tavira:

Tavira Youth Hostel: This centrally situated hostel provides private and dormitory accommodations, making it perfect for budget-conscious guests. It also has a shared kitchen where visitors may make meals and common rooms for socializing.

HI Tavira - Pousada de Juventude: Part of the Portuguese youth hostel network, this hostel offers inexpensive lodging with minimal facilities and is popular with younger tourists.

Hostels are ideal for folks who want a more social setting and do not mind sharing space with other visitors.

3. Guest houses (pensões e residenciais)

Budget: €30 to €80 each night.

Guesthouses, also known as Pensões and Residenciais, are modest, family-run institutions that provide an intimate and customized experience. These accommodations are comparable to bed-and-breakfasts, offering a comfortable stay with greater contact with the hosts, who are often locals.

Tavira's guest houses vary from simple rooms with communal bathrooms to more opulent accommodations with en-suite amenities. They are usually found in or around the town center, making it simple to explore Tavira on foot. Some guest houses provide breakfast at their overnight rates.

Recommended guesthouses in Tavira:

Calcada Guesthouse is a beautifully renovated guest house in Tavira's old district that offers comfortable rooms with contemporary conveniences and an outside patio.
Casa Beleza do Sul is a beautiful hotel with traditional architecture and breathtaking views of the river and town. It's ideal for couples looking for a romantic, tranquil getaway.
Guesthouses are perfect for individuals seeking a local experience since the proprietors typically provide customized insights and recommendations.

4. Bed and Breakfast (B&Bs)

Budget: €40 to €100 each night.

Bed and breakfasts, or B&Bs, are a great alternative to hotels. B&Bs, like guesthouses, provide a comfortable setting with the extra benefit of a prepared breakfast every morning. Tavira's bed and breakfasts vary from historic townhouses to rural residences, with many providing a warm and friendly atmosphere.

A bed and breakfast is ideal for couples or lone tourists seeking a relaxing setting. The hosts are frequently happy to offer local expertise and may assist with activity planning, making your stay more customized and engaging.

Notable Bed & Breakfasts in Tavira:

Tavira Terrace: A lovely bed and breakfast with a rooftop terrace that provides panoramic views of the city. It's near the town center and has a comfortable but classy atmosphere.
Casa do Rio Tavira Inn: This bed and breakfast on the riverbank provides stunning views and a calm ambiance. The accommodations are attractively designed, and the pleasant hosts provide good area suggestions.

5. Camping & Glamping

Budget: €10 to €60 each night.

Camping or glamping (luxury camping) is an excellent option for nature enthusiasts or those looking for a more adventurous experience. Tavira is adjacent to various natural parks and beaches, providing enough outdoor area for camping.

Camping:

Camping Tavira: Located near the Ria Formosa Natural Park, this campground offers basic tent camping amenities including bathrooms, showers, and picnic spots. It's great for folks who appreciate spending time outside and want to keep on a tight budget.

Glamping:

Luxury Glamping Tavira: For those who wish to enjoy the outdoors without compromising luxury, glamping is an elegant option. Glamping locations include well-furnished tents with facilities such as comfy mattresses, private toilets, and air conditioning.

Camping is the most affordable alternative, whilst glamping provides a more luxury, nature-based experience.

6. Agriturismo (Farmstays)

Budget: €50 to €120 per night.

Agriturismo, sometimes known as farm stays, refers to rural lodgings situated on working farms. Farm stays in Tavira and nearby regions provide a one-of-a-kind chance to experience the agricultural culture of the Algarve. Guests may often participate in agricultural activities such as fruit harvesting, animal care, and even learning traditional culinary skills.

Staying on a farm provides a calm escape from city life as well as the opportunity to immerse yourself in local culture and scenery. This sort of lodging is ideal for families, couples, and lone visitors looking to experience rural life in Portugal.

Recommended Farmstays:

Quinta Dos Perfumes: Nestled in the Tavira countryside, this lovely farm stay provides elegant rooms surrounded by citrus groves. Guests may enjoy organic breakfasts, nature hikes, and the peacefulness of the countryside.
Quinta Almargem Lusitano: A tranquil rural hotel nestled in a nature reserve, providing farm-fresh meals, horseback riding, and breathtaking views of the Algarve's hills.

Tavira has a broad range of alternative lodging alternatives in addition to regular hotels, appealing to a variety of interests and budgets. Tavira offers something for everyone, whether you want to stay in a magnificent villa, a quiet guesthouse, or a low-cost hostel. By selecting the appropriate lodging type for your requirements, you may improve your trip experience while keeping expenses under control.

Essential Transportation Choices for Tourists.

When planning a vacation to Tavira, Portugal, considering the available transportation choices is critical to ensure a seamless and pleasurable experience. Tavira, a picturesque town in the Algarve area, has a variety of transportation options to suit different budgets and interests. Whether you're going inside Tavira or touring the neighboring regions, here's a thorough reference to crucial transportation alternatives

1. Walking is the best way to explore Tavira's Old Town.

Budget: free.
Recommended routes: Historic Center, Roman Bridge, Tavira Castle, and Praça da República.

Walking is one of the most comfortable methods to discover Tavira. The town's small size makes it simple to traverse and strolling lets you explore its attractive cobblestone streets, ancient buildings, and bustling squares at your leisure. The majority of Tavira's main attractions, including the Roman Bridge, Tavira Castle, and the town's several churches, are in or near the historic center, making walking the preferred mode of transportation for touring.

Benefits of Walking:

- Walking is free, making it the most cost-effective alternative.
- Convenient: Tavira's streets, including the Praça da República, are constructed for pedestrian traffic.
- Immersive Experience: Walking enables travelers to thoroughly absorb the town's rich history, architecture, and local culture while stopping at cafés and stores.

2. Bicycle Rentals

Budget: €10 to €20 each day.
Best Routes: Tavira to Santa Luzia (to Barril Beach), Ria Formosa Natural Park, and adjacent communities

For those who prefer riding, renting a bicycle is an excellent way to navigate Tavira and explore the surrounding region. The town is generally level, making it simple to pedal between locations. Tourists like the cycling path that leads to Santa Luzia, a little fishing community approximately 3 kilometers from Tavira known for its octopus dishes and scenic Barril Beach. You may also ride through the Ria Formosa Natural Park, a breathtaking coastal lagoon system teeming with animals.

Bike Rental Options:

EcoBike Tavira: Rents conventional and electric bikes beginning at €10 per day for ordinary bikes and €20 per day for electric bikes.
CicloSport Tavira: Another bike rental business with low daily prices and a variety of bike models available.

Benefits of Cycling:

- Cycling is ideal for individuals who want an active method to experience the town and its surrounding attractions.
- Eco-Friendly: Cycling has no environmental effect and is a greener mode of transportation.
- Cost-effective: Bike rentals are less costly than other forms of transportation, and they allow you to visit locations that are difficult to get by automobile.

3. The public bus system

Budget: €2-€5 each ride.
Best routes: Tavira to Faro, Olhão, e Cabanas.

Tavira's public bus system, run by EVA Transportes, links the town to other towns and villages, making it an affordable alternative for visitors visiting the Algarve area. Buses go often to places like Faro and Olhão, as well as the adjacent community of Cabanas, which is noted for its magnificent beach and peaceful attitude. Bus prices are generally reasonable, ranging from €2 to €5, depending on the distance traveled.

Main bus routes:

- Tavira to Faro: A 45-minute ride brings you to the Algarve's capital, Faro, which offers better transit connections and an international airport.
- From Tavira, take a short bus journey to Olhão, a historic fishing town known for its seafood and market.
- Tavira to Cabanas: A fast trip to the adjacent community of Cabanas, which provides access to Cabanas Beach and other water sports.

Benefits of Public Buses:

- Inexpensive: The bus system is one of the most economical modes of transportation in Tavira, particularly for visits to adjacent towns.
- Extensive Routes: The buses allow access to areas that are inaccessible on foot or by bike, such as adjacent cities and beaches.
- Good for Longer Distances: While walking and cycling are great ways to get to Tavira, buses are preferable for traveling to other parts of the Algarve.

4. Taxis

Budget: €5-€15 for short journeys within Tavira; €30-€40 for longer travels (e.g., to Faro).
Route: Tavira's best routes include those to surrounding beaches, Santa Luzia, and the train station.

Taxis are an excellent choice for travelers who want direct, hassle-free transportation, particularly when traveling with baggage or when public transit timetables are difficult. Taxis in Tavira use a metered system and may be located at taxi stops around the town or summoned by phone or mobile applications such as Bolt.

Approximate taxi costs:
Tavira to Barril Beach: Around €10 to €15.

Tavira to Faro Airport: around €30 to €40, depending on traffic.

Tavira to Tavira Island Ferry Terminal: Costs between €5 and €7 for a fast voyage to the island.

Benefits of Using Taxis:

- Convenience: Taxis provide door-to-door service, which is especially handy for passengers with large bags or who are going late at night.
- Comfort: Taxis are air-conditioned and provide a more intimate experience than buses.
- Taxis, unlike buses, run around the clock, making them available at all times.

5. Train:

Budget: €3 to €7 for each trip.

Best Routes: Tavira to Faro, Vila Real de Santo António, and Tavira to Lagos.

Tavira's train station links the town to the rest of the Algarve via the regional rail service run by Comboios de Portugal (CP). The Algarve Line runs from east to west along the coast, connecting several of the region's major resorts. Trains are a fantastic alternative for travelers looking to travel beyond Tavira and see towns like Faro,

Lagos, and Vila Real de Santo António. Train costs are low, with short excursions costing between €3 and €7.

Main Train Routes:

- Tavira to Faro: A 40-minute rail travel costing about €3.50, ideal for day visits to the Algarve's capital.
- Tavira to Vila Real de Santo António: A 25-minute rail trip costs roughly €3 and takes you to the border town with Spain.
- Tavira to Lagos is a lengthier two-hour excursion that costs roughly €7.

Benefits of taking the train:

- Picturesque Views: The Algarve Line follows the coast, providing picturesque views of the sea, landscape, and small villages along the route.
- Trains are a pleasant and cost-effective method to travel vast distances without dealing with traffic or parking.
- Access to Major Towns: The rail links Tavira to numerous major towns in the Algarve, making it perfect for travelers looking to explore the area without hiring a vehicle.

6. Ferries

Budget: €1.50 to €2.50 for each ride.

The best routes are Tavira to Tavira Island and Tavira to Cabanas Island.

Ferries are a vital mode of transportation for visitors visiting Tavira, especially those who want to explore the adjacent islands. The most popular boat route connects Tavira's Quatro Águas port to Tavira Island, a gorgeous beach location. Cabanas Island, another lovely beach spot, is also accessible by ferry. Ferry fares are modest, ranging from €1.50 to €2.50 per trip, and provide a picturesque route over the Ria Formosa lagoon.

Ferry routes:

Tavira to Tavira Island: A 15-minute journey costs around €2 per person.

Tavira to Cabanas Island: Another short journey, costing between €1.50 and €2, with boats going often throughout the day.

Benefits of Taking Ferry:

- Direct Access to Beaches: Ferries are the only means to get to Tavira Island and Cabanas Island, hence they are vital for beachgoers.
- Ferry fares are inexpensive, even for families and groups.

- Scenic Journeys: The boat routes provide wonderful views of the Ria Formosa Natural Park, which enhances the whole experience.

7. Car rentals

Budget: €25 - €60 per day (rental); €1.60 per liter of petrol.
Best routes: Tavira to Faro, Tavira to Lagos, and Tavira to interior communities.

Renting a vehicle gives you the greatest freedom to explore Tavira and the surrounding Algarve area. While a car is not required to navigate Tavira's town center, it is beneficial if you want to explore more secluded beaches, interior villages, or other Algarve cities at your leisure. Car rentals in Tavira cost between €25 and €60 per day, depending on the kind of car and rental operator. Prices might vary depending on the season, so reserving in advance is recommended, particularly during high tourist months.

Car Rental Companies:

Sixt Car Rental, located in Tavira, provides a selection of automobiles beginning at about €25 per day.

Europcar Tavira offers cheap pricing and excellent customer service, with rates beginning at roughly €30 per day.

Advantages of Car Rentals:

- Convenience: Renting a vehicle allows travelers to quickly visit off-the-beaten-path sites like the magnificent beaches of Praia do Barril and Praia da Ilha de Tavira.
- Freedom: Having a vehicle enables you to choose your route and travel at your leisure, free from the constraints of public transit timetables.
- Access to Nearby Attractions: Many stunning locations in the Algarve, such as the lovely villages of Lagos and Silves, are more easily accessible by automobile.

Tavira has a choice of transportation alternatives to suit various interests and budgets. Whether you choose to walk around the lovely neighborhoods, bike to neighboring beaches, or hire a vehicle for a more in-depth study of the Algarve area, there is a way of transportation for everyone.

Walking and bicycling are ideal for leisurely local exploration, while buses and trains offer cost-effective transportation to distant towns. Taxis and rental automobiles are convenient and flexible, especially for those vacationing with family or wanting to explore more distant destinations.

Chapter 5
Popular Tourist Attractions in Tavira

T he region has a combination of clean sandy coasts and attractive surroundings, making it a perfect beach resort. Here's a comprehensive guide to Tavira's principal beaches, including their locations, admission prices, and what to anticipate when you visit.

1. Tavira's island beach

Location: A short boat journey from Tavira, leaving from Quatro Águas.

Entry Fee: A round-trip ferry ticket costs around €2.50 per passenger.

Praia da Ilha de Tavira is one of the region's most popular beaches, with a lengthy stretch of fine sand and clean seas. The beach is backed by a protected area of dunes and flora, creating a stunning natural backdrop. The facilities include beach bars and restaurants, as well as loungers and umbrellas for hire.

What To Expect:

Activities include swimming, sunbathing, and water activities like paddleboarding and kayaking. There are also walking pathways in the adjacent natural park.

Family-Friendly: The beach is suitable for children, with shallow waters and lifeguards on duty during peak season.

2. Barra do Barril

Location: On the eastern side of Tavira Island, accessible via boat or a picturesque stroll from the parking lot.

Entry Fee: The ferry to the beach costs around €2.50. There is no extra charge for the beach itself.

This beach is well-known for its peaceful environment and attractive surroundings, which include a unique anchor cemetery—an artwork of rusted anchors that commemorates the area's fishing past. The beach is well-kept and has a variety of services, including showers, restaurants, and beach rentals.

What To Expect:

Activities: Ideal for leisure, sunbathing, and swimming, with a picturesque view of the shore. The neighborhood also contains bike routes for individuals who want to explore the neighboring scenery.

Quiet Vibe: Because it is less congested than other beaches, it is a popular destination for individuals seeking peace.

3. Cabanas beach.

Location: Near the town of Cabanas de Tavira, about 4 kilometers from Tavira, and accessible by a short boat trip from Cabanas.

Access price: The boat ride costs around €1.50 per person for a round journey, and there is no access price to the beach.

Praia de Cabanas is a family-friendly beach with smooth, golden sand and shallow seas. The beach is dotted with attractive restaurants and cafés, ideal for a dinner or a drink after sunbathing.

What To Expect:

Family-friendly: The gradual slope of the beach and shallow seas are ideal for children, with plenty of room to construct sandcastles.

Local Dining: Visitors may eat fresh seafood at the local beach bars.

4. Tavira Island's Forte beach

Location: This beach is near the fort on Tavira Island and may be reached by the same ferry that travels to Praia da Ilha de Tavira.

Entry Fee: Like Ilha de Tavira, the ferry costs roughly €2.50 for a round ride.

This beach, known for its rich history, is next to a medieval fort and provides stunning views of the Atlantic. The beach boasts smooth sand, clean seas, and a more private environment.

What To Expect:

Historical Interest: Because of its closeness to the fort, this location is ideal for history buffs.

Relaxation: With fewer people, the sunbathing and swimming areas are more calm.

5. Terra Estreita beach

Location: Reachable from the beach by walking or cycling along a nature trail, or by boat from Tavira.

Access Fee: There is no admission charge; however, transportation expenses apply if you use a boat.

This beach is more remote, offering a natural and untouched setting. It has good beaches and a gorgeous environment, which is ideal for nature enthusiasts.

What To Expect:

Serene Environment: Ideal for individuals seeking to avoid the busier beaches.

Nature Trails: Use walking routes to explore the local environment and see animals.

6. Praia da Marina

Location: About a 30-minute drive from Tavira, near Carvoeiro.

Entry Fee: Free, although parking may cost between €2 and €3.

Praia da Marinha is one of the most beautiful beaches in the Algarve, with spectacular cliffs, crystal-clear seas, and breathtaking vistas. Although it is a little farther from Tavira, the natural beauty makes the trek worthwhile.

What To Expect:

Scenic Beauty: Ideal for photography, swimming, and snorkeling. The unusual rock formations make it a popular destination for nature lovers.

Facilities: There are few facilities, although some neighboring eateries welcome guests.

7. Beach of Tesos

Location: On the western part of Tavira Island, accessible by boat from Tavira.

Entry Fee: Around €2.50 for the boat voyage.

This beach is recognized for its large sandy sections and quiet waves, which make it ideal for a variety of water sports. It is less popular with visitors, allowing for a more relaxed atmosphere.

What To Expect:

Water Sports: Excellent for kayaking and paddleboarding.

Relaxed Atmosphere: An ideal location for individuals wishing to unwind away from the throng.

8. Praia da Algoa

Location: Approximately 7 kilometers from Tavira, near Altura, and readily accessible by automobile.

Entry fee: free; parking may be provided for a nominal cost.

This beach is well-known for its family-friendly ambiance and services, which include restaurants, loungers, and beach bars.

What To Expect:

Family-friendly: Safe swimming conditions and lots of room for kids to play.

Local Amenities: Facilities include baths and restaurants, making it ideal for day visits.

9. Praia da Fabrica

Location: It is located in the Ria Formosa Natural Park, just outside of Tavira.

Access Fee: There are no fees for admission, although transportation expenses may apply.

Praia da Fábrica is known for its serene environment and magnificent natural beauty, and it is frequently less crowded, providing a pleasant beach experience. The beach has a blend of sandy sand and natural surroundings.

What To Expect:

Natural Beauty: An ideal location for nature enthusiasts and photographers.

Quiet Space: Less touristy, making it excellent for unwinding.

10. Praia da Lota

Location: Around 9 kilometers from Tavira, in the settlement of Cabanas de Tavira.

Entry fee: free; parking may be provided for a nominal cost.

Praia da Lota is recognized for its magnificent cliffs and crystal-clear seas, which make it a popular swimming and sunbathing destination. Visitors to the beach may dine at one of the numerous beach bars and restaurants.

What To Expect:

Beautiful vistas: The spectacular cliffs provide stunning vistas and fantastic photographic opportunities.

Showers and beach rentals are available, providing enough facilities for a relaxing beach day.

Historical Sites and Monuments

Tavira is a lovely town in Portugal's Algarve area with a rich history and culture. Its historical landmarks and monuments illustrate the many influences that have affected the region throughout time, including Roman colonies, Moorish construction, and Christian reconquest. Here's an in-depth look at some of Tavira's most important historical landmarks and monuments, emphasizing their significance and peculiarities.

1. Tavira Castle (Castelo de Tavira).

Tavira Castle, perched on a hilltop, was built in the 11th century by the Moors. The castle, originally designed as a defensive fortification, was strategically vital owing to its position, which overlooked the town and the surrounding countryside.

Features:

Architecture: The castle's walls include a variety of architectural styles, including Moorish and later Gothic influences. Visitors may view the castle walls, various watchtowers, and a lovely garden on the castle grounds.

Views: The castle provides breathtaking panoramic views of Tavira, the river, and the surrounding countryside, making it a favorite photographic location.

Visiting Information:

Tavira Castle is open to the public and is often featured in guided tours of the town. There is no admission price, and it offers an interesting look into the region's past.

2. Saint Bonfim's Church

This Baroque church, constructed in the 18th century, is one of Tavira's most prominent religious landmarks. Its impressive façade and detailed interior make it a must-see for anybody interested in religious architecture.

Features:

Interior: The church is ornamented with exquisite azulejos (ceramic tiles) representing scenes from Christ's life, as well as elaborate gilded altarpieces.

Cultural Significance: The church is still functioning today, with regular services and community activities, adding to its significance in local culture.

Visiting Information:

Igreja do Senhor do Bonfim is usually available to the public throughout the day, and visitors are invited to attend services or tour the interior.

3. Igreja Santa Maria do Castelo

This church, originally erected in the 13th century, was built on the site of a medieval mosque when Tavira was reconquered by Christians. It marks the region's shift from Moorish to Christian architectural styles.

Features:

Architecture: The church is a mix of Gothic and Manueline styles, with a lovely façade and elaborate embellishments on the interior.
Historical significance: The chapel includes the burial of Francisco Rodrigues Lobo, a great 16th-century Portuguese poet and significant figure in Portuguese literature.

Visiting Information:

The church welcomes tourists, and there is usually a nominal charge to access the main area. It is a tranquil area to contemplate Tavira's historical importance.

4. Roman Bridge (Old Bridge on the Gilão River).

Tavira's Roman Bridge, built in the third century AD, is a spectacular example of ancient engineering. It was designed to link both banks of the River Gilão and is now one of the town's prominent sights.

Features:

Structure: The bridge is made up of many limestone arches and is well-known for its durability.
Historical Significance: The bridge was an important crossing point in antiquity, aiding commerce and transit across the area.

Visiting Information:
The bridge is free to explore and provides stunning views of the river and town. It is often the starting point for walking tours of Tavira.

5. Tavira Municipal Museum (Musée Municipal de Tavira)

The Tavira Municipal Museum, housed in a former convent, commemorates the town's and surrounding area's rich history. It has an extensive collection of antiquities from numerous historical periods, including Roman and Moorish times.

Features:

Exhibits: The museum houses archeological artifacts, religious art, and exhibitions that tell the narrative of Tavira and its cultural legacy.

Architecture: The building is a historical landmark, with stunning courtyards and architectural characteristics reminiscent of its history as a monastery.

Visiting Information:

The museum is open all year and normally charges a nominal admission fee. Those interested in learning more about Tavira's history may take guided excursions.

6. Tavira Municipal Council (Town Hall).

The Tavira Town Hall, situated in the town's historic center, is a stunning example of 18th-century architecture. It plays an important part in the town's administration.

Features:

Facade: The building's neoclassical architecture has exquisite columns and ornamental accents.

Historical Role: For generations, the Town Hall has served as the seat of municipal government and remains a focus of communal activity.

Visiting Information:

Visitors may tour the outside of the structure and often enter the inside to see local art exhibits or cultural activities.

7. Convento Nossa Senhora da Graça

This old convent, constructed in the sixteenth century, symbolizes Tavira's religious heritage. It has undergone various alterations throughout the years, and it is now a cultural center and a significant monument.

Features:

The convent's architecture combines Manueline and Baroque styles, including stunning altarpieces and cloisters.

Cultural Activities: The convent is an active member of the local community, hosting art exhibits, cultural events, and concerts on a regular basis.

Visiting Information:

Access to the convent is normally available during exhibits and events, with an admission cost depending on the occasion.

8. Ponte de Tavira (Tavira Bridge).

The Tavira Bridge, often known as the "New Bridge," is a contemporary construction that serves to complement the Roman Bridge. It is an important pedestrian crossing across the River Gilão.

Features:

The bridge is meant to fit in with the town's historical aspects while yet offering contemporary utility.
Accessibility: It links several regions of Tavira, allowing tourists to easily explore the area.
Visiting Information:

As a pedestrian bridge, there is no admission cost, and it is a lovely stroll for people touring Tavira.

9. Quinta Da Ria

Quinta da Ria is largely recognized as a golf resort, but it also has historical value, dating back to the region's agricultural history. The estate has typical Portuguese architecture and magnificent grounds.

Features:

Architecture: The estate has classic Algarve architecture, such as whitewashed walls and terracotta roofs.
Cultural significance: It showcases Tavira's agricultural legacy and adjacent surroundings, offering insight into traditional farming processes.

Visiting Information:

The estate is available to the public, and visitors may enjoy the grounds while learning about the area's agricultural heritage.

10. Cacela Velha Fort (Forte da Cacela)

The Cacela Velha Fort, located within a short drive from Tavira, was built in the 16th century and provides insight into the region's military history. It was intended to defend the shoreline from pirates and intruders.

Features:

Views: The fort is built on a cliff, offering breathtaking views of the Atlantic Ocean and the surrounding terrain. Historical significance: The fort played an important part in the defense of the Algarve and is an exceptional example of military construction from the medieval period.

Visiting Information:

The fort is free to visit, and it draws a large number of people interested in history and photography.

Outdoor Activities in Tavira

Tavira, located in the picturesque Algarve region of Portugal, is not only known for its rich history and charming architecture but also for a wide array of outdoor activities that cater to all types of travelers. Whether you're an adventure seeker, a nature lover, or someone looking to relax by the beach, Tavira has something for everyone.

1. Beach Activities.

Tavira is home to some of the most beautiful beaches in the Algarve, making it an ideal location for sunbathing, swimming, and water sports.

Praia do Barril: This beach is famed for its smooth sands and clean seas. Visitors may enjoy swimming, sunbathing, or visiting the neighboring nudist beach. The beach can be reached by a picturesque train ride or a short walk over the dunes.

Water Sports: Many beaches, notably Praia do Barril and Praia de Cacela Velha, provide equipment rentals for kayaking, paddleboarding, and windsurfing. Local firms give instruction for novices, making it simple for everyone to participate.

2. Hikes & Nature Walks

The natural splendor of Tavira offers several chances for hiking and nature hikes, with routes leading through stunning landscapes, hills, and sea vistas.

Ria Formosa Natural Park: With its diverse ecosystems, including marshes, lagoons, and sandy islands, it's a great spot for birdwatching and hiking. There are marked trails that offer stunning views and the opportunity to see various species of birds, especially during migration seasons.

Via Algarviana: This long-distance walking track goes from the Spanish border to Cape St. Vincent, and a piece of it passes near Tavira, giving walkers an opportunity to see the Algarve's agricultural nature, which includes picturesque towns, hills, and breathtaking views.

3. Cycling and Mountain Biking.

Tavira is a fantastic location for cycling aficionados, with multiple bike rental businesses and several picturesque paths to explore.

The EcoVia do Litoral is a popular route that goes along the coastline and offers spectacular views of the water. There are various easy roads along the coast and more demanding trails in the hills, making it appropriate for both leisurely rides and serious mountain riding.

Guided excursions: For those who prefer a guided experience, many local firms provide bicycle excursions through Tavira's countryside, wineries, and lesser-known locations.

4. Bird-watching
Tavira's distinct habitats make it an ideal location for birding.

The Ria Formosa Natural Park is known for its bird species, including flamingos, herons, and numerous migratory birds. Many local tour companies provide birdwatching trips, which include binoculars and knowledge to help you find and identify the different species.

Activities: Local naturalists conduct birding activities and seminars for guests to learn more about the area's biodiversity and conservation efforts.

5. Fishing

Fishing is a popular outdoor activity in Tavira, owing to the abundant marine life.

Tourists may try their hand at sea fishing or freshwater fishing in adjacent rivers. Many local operators provide fishing charters that take you out into the Atlantic for a day of angling, where you can catch species such as sea bass, bream, and mackerel.

Local Knowledge: Many charter companies give all of the essential equipment and even advise on the best tactics to utilize.

6. Golfing

Tavira has numerous great golf courses situated against breathtaking settings.

Quinta da Ria Golf Course: This course is noted for its stunning views of the Ria Formosa and the mountains. It has demanding holes and well-maintained greens, making it a favorite among both residents and visitors.

Golf Packages: Many Tavira hotels provide golf packages that include lodging, food, and tee times, making it a simple way to spend a golfing vacation.

7. Boat tours and excursions.

Exploring Tavira from the boat is an excellent way to experience its coastline splendor.

River Cruises: Tour companies provide calm boat journeys down the River Gilão, affording breathtaking views of Tavira's old center from a new viewpoint. These cruises sometimes include stops at beaches and islands for swimming or relaxation.

Tavira Island and Cacela Velha Island are popular destinations for boat cruises that involve swimming, sunbathing, and exploration of beautiful natural surroundings.

8. Horseback Riding.

For those looking for a fresh viewpoint on the Algarve, horseback riding is an excellent outdoor activity.

Riding trips: Several equestrian facilities around Tavira arrange guided horseback trips through the countryside and along the shore, which are suitable for all skill levels and provide a calm opportunity to discover the region's natural beauty.

Tavira offers a wide range of outdoor activities for tourists looking to explore the beauty of the Algarve, from beach days and hiking adventures to birdwatching and cultural experiences, there's something for everyone. Whether you're looking for relaxation or adventure, Tavira's outdoor offerings will ensure a memorable experience.

Chapter 6

Top Tavira Tourist Foods with Health Benefits

Tavira, located in Portugal's Algarve region, is a culinary treasure that offers visitors a rich tapestry of flavors rooted in its diverse cultural heritage. From fresh seafood to hearty stews, Tavira's cuisine reflects its coastal geography and agricultural richness.

1. Seafood dishes.

Grilled Sardines (Sardinhas Assadas)

Grilled sardines are a hallmark of Portuguese cuisine, particularly in coastal places like Tavira. These little fish are often seasoned with salt and grilled over an open flame, producing a smokey, rich taste.

Health Benefits:

- Sardines are high in omega-3 fatty acids, which are good for your heart, lower inflammation, and improve cognitive function.
- Sardines are high in protein and aid with muscle repair and development.

2. Salada de Polvo (Tavira's Octopus Salad).

This meal consists of a soft octopus that has been cooked and marinated in olive oil, vinegar, onions, and bell peppers, resulting in a delicious salad ideal for warm days.

Health Benefits:

- Low Calories: Octopus is low in calories but rich in protein, making it an ideal option for people trying to maintain a healthy weight.
- Nutrient-dense: It includes essential vitamins and minerals such as vitamin B12, iron, and magnesium, all of which improve general health and energy levels.

3. Cataplana de Marisco, or Seafood Cataplana

This classic seafood meal is prepared in a distinctive copper pot known as a cataplana, including a combination of fresh fish, shellfish, and fragrant vegetables. The ingredients are steamed together, enabling the flavors to blend nicely.

Health Benefits:

- Tomatoes, garlic, and herbs are high in antioxidants, which help protect the body from oxidative stress.
- Heart-Healthy: Combining fish with olive oil promotes a heart-healthy diet.

4. Bacalhau à Brás (Brás Codfish).

Bacalhau, or salt cod, is a popular element in Portuguese cuisine; in this recipe, it is shredded and combined with onions, garlic, and potatoes, then bound with scrambled eggs.

Health Benefits:

- High in Protein: Salt cod has a lot of protein, which is necessary for muscle repair and development.
- Cod, like sardines, contains omega-3 fatty acids, which are essential to heart and brain health.

5. Tavira Cheese (Queijo de Tavira).

Tavira is well-known for its artisanal cheese, which is prepared from sheep's milk and typically matured to create rich tastes. It may be consumed on its own or with local bread and olives.

Health Benefits:

- Calcium is an important mineral for bone health, and cheese is a good supply of it.
- Probiotics: Certain kinds include helpful microorganisms that promote intestinal health.

6. Piri-piri chicken (Frango Piri-piri).

This meal, which originated in Portuguese cuisine, comprises marinated chicken that is grilled and served with a spicy piri-piri sauce. It is a popular option in Tavira and provides a delightful experience.

Health Benefits:

- Lean Protein: Chicken contains lean protein, which is essential for muscle maintenance and general health.
- Metabolism Booster: Piri-piri sauce contains spices, notably chile, that may help with metabolism and digestion.

7. Algarve-Style Vegetable Stew (Migas).

Migas, a typical Portuguese dish cooked with leftover bread, garlic, and seasonal vegetables, depicts the region's rustic culinary style while offering a substantial and full supper.

Health Benefits:

- High in Fiber: Whole grain bread and veggies have more fiber, which promotes digestive health.
- The meal is nutrient-dense due to the variety of veggies utilized.

8. Custard Tarts (Pasteis de Nata)

While not exclusive to Tavira, these classic Portuguese pastries are widely accessible and adored by visitors. They have a creamy custard filling in a flaky pastry shell and are often topped with cinnamon and powdered sugar.

Health Benefits:

- Moderation is key: While these snacks are heavy in sugar and fat, eating them on occasion might fulfill a sweet appetite without fully derailing a balanced diet.
- Calcium Source: The custard is produced with milk, thus it contains calcium.

9. Algarve Wine

The Algarve area is recognized for producing a range of wines, including reds, whites, and rosés. Many local wineries provide tastings, enabling travelers to sample the region's tastes firsthand.

Health Benefits:

- Antioxidants: Moderate wine drinking, particularly red wine, has been linked to improved heart health owing to its antioxidant characteristics.
- Cultural Experience: Wine tasting offers a glimpse into the local culture and customs.

10. Fresh fruit and nuts

Tavira's markets are brimming with fresh, locally produced fruits including figs, almonds, and oranges, which may be eaten as snacks or utilized in a variety of meals.

Health Benefits:

- Nutrient-dense: Fresh fruits are abundant in vitamins, minerals, and antioxidants, which promote general health.

- Healthy Fats: Nuts are high in healthy fats, protein, and fiber, making them an ideal healthy snack option.

11. Chouriço (Portuguese sausage).

Chouriço is a classic Portuguese sausage that is commonly eaten grilled or in stews. Its smokey taste lends depth to many meals.

Health Benefits:

- Protein Source: Chouriço is an excellent source of protein, which is required for muscle upkeep.
- Flavorful Experience: Although it should be used in moderation owing to its fat level, its rich taste makes it a favorite ingredient in many meals.

Tavira's flavors will undoubtedly leave a lasting impression, whether you're dining at a local restaurant or attempting to cook them yourself. By sampling these dishes, visitors can embark on a flavorful journey that nourishes the body while immersing themselves in the vibrant culture of Tavira.

Top Restaurants in Tavira

1. Restaurante O Pescador.

Located by the river, O Pescador specializes in fresh seafood meals and traditional Portuguese cuisine. The restaurant's design is modest but appealing, with an emphasis on offering a genuine eating experience.

Signature dishes:

Grilled Sardines: A local delicacy that's simply seasoned and cooked to perfection.
Seafood Cataplana is a delicious seafood stew that embodies the flavor of the Algarve.

Ambiance:
O Pescador, with its casual environment and helpful staff, is excellent for families and couples searching for a true Tavira experience.

Pricing Range:
Moderate, with main meals often ranging between €10 and €20.

2. A ver Tavira

Perched on a hill, A Ver Tavira provides spectacular views of the town and the surrounding countryside, combining native tastes with modern cooking methods.

Signature dishes:

Octopus Salad is a refreshing meal with well-balanced tastes.
Piri-Piri Chicken: Grilled to perfection, this meal is a must-try for spice enthusiasts.

Ambiance:
The modern décor and stunning vistas provide a romantic atmosphere ideal for special events.

Pricing Range:
meals range between €15 and €30.

3. Restaurante Bica

Restaurante Bica is noted for its traditional Portuguese cuisine presented in a pleasant, rustic setting. The emphasis is on local ingredients and historic recipes.

Signature dishes:

Bacalhau à Brás is a traditional Portuguese comfort dish consisting of salted fish, onions, potatoes, and eggs.
Algarve Vegetable Stew: A wonderful and substantial recipe that highlights the region's products.

Ambiance:

Bica's warm, friendly ambiance makes it ideal for a relaxed supper with friends or family.

Pricing Range:
Main courses are reasonably priced, ranging from €8 to €15.

4. Restaurante 7 São Sebastião

7 São Sebastião is a restaurant recognized for its unique approach to classic Portuguese cuisine. The cooks use fresh, locally sourced ingredients.

Signature dishes:

Lamb Shank: Slow-cooked till tender and served with fresh veggies.
Fish of the Day: Always fresh and served with a distinctive touch.

Ambiance:
The restaurant's sleek, contemporary décor provides a sophisticated yet pleasant eating experience.

Pricing Range:
Moderate to high, with entrees ranging from €12 to €28.

5. Tasca de Abade

Tasca do Abade, a hidden treasure in Tavira, provides a comfortable and easygoing ambiance in which visitors may savor genuine Portuguese tapas.

Signature dishes:

Cheese and Charcuterie Boards are ideal for sharing and showcasing local specialties.
Pork Alentejana is a classic meal with pork and clams in a delicious sauce.

Ambiance:
Tasca do Abade's laid-back feel makes it perfect for a relaxing lunch with friends and superb wine.

Pricing Range:
Tapas are inexpensive, ranging between €5 to €10.

6. Restaurante Casa Do Castelo

Casa do Castelo, located near the Tavira castle, serves a delicious combination of traditional and contemporary meals made with high-quality ingredients.

Signature dishes:

Duck Rice is a tasty meal that showcases local ingredients.
Seafood Rice is a rich, substantial meal ideal for seafood lovers.

Ambiance:
The rustic design and breathtaking vistas make it an ideal place for a relaxing supper.

Pricing Range:
Moderate, with most main meals ranging from €10 to €20.

7. O Bistrô do Chefe

This café exemplifies current culinary expertise, serving a variety of meals that combine worldwide inspirations with Portuguese traditions.

Signature dishes:

Tuna Tartare: Fresh and nicely prepared, highlighting the chef's abilities.
Pork Tenderloin: Perfectly cooked and presented with unique side dishes.

Ambiance:

Bistro do Chefe's contemporary design and dynamic atmosphere make it ideal for foodies seeking a great dining experience.

Pricing Range:
Moderate to expensive, with meals ranging between €12 and €25.

8. Restaurante O Marisco.

O Marisco, as the name implies, specializes in seafood meals that are prepared using traditional techniques and fresh ingredients.

Signature dishes:

Bulhão Pato are steamed clams served with garlic and cilantro.
Seafood Platter: A sampling of the Algarve's freshest catches.

Ambiance:
The informal, maritime-themed design makes it an enjoyable destination for seafood enthusiasts.

Pricing Range:
Moderate, with main meals often ranging between €10 and €20.

9. Pizzeria Baffi

For those searching for an alternative to traditional Portuguese food, Pizzaria Baffi serves exquisite wood-fired pizzas cooked with fresh ingredients.

Signature dishes:

Margherita Pizza: Classic tastes and a beautiful crust.
Seafood Pizza: A one-of-a-kind innovation that incorporates local seafood.

Ambiance:
Casual and family-friendly, it's an excellent choice for a relaxing evening out.

Pricing Range:
Pizzas are inexpensive, usually between €7 and €15.

10. Restaurante Ria Formosa

This restaurant, located in the Ria Formosa Natural Park, is well-known for its magnificent views and devotion to serving fresh, local fish.

Signature dishes:

Grilled Fish: Always a fresh catch, simply cooked to bring out its inherent tastes.

Seafood Spaghetti: A delicious combination of tastes and textures.

Ambiance:

The magnificent vistas and outdoor dining provide the ideal atmosphere for a memorable supper.

Pricing Range:

The main meals range from €10 to €25.

Chapter 7

Local Crafts and Souvenirs

Tourists visiting Tavira may discover the region's unique artisan culture, which represents its cultural past. Tavira sells a wide range of products, from handcrafted pottery to traditional fabrics, that make ideal travel souvenirs. Here, let's look at the local crafts and souvenirs available in Tavira:

1. Ceramics

Ceramics are one of the most prominent local crafts in Tavira, showcasing the region's creative flare and cultural history. The town's ceramics are generally brightly colored and intricately designed, drawing inspiration from the classic patterns seen on Portuguese tiles (azules).

Key features:

Traditional Patterns: Many ceramics have geometric patterns or floral themes that are typical of Algarve art. Functional and ornamental goods: Ceramic goods range from tableware and service dishes to ornamental tiles and wall hangings.

Where to Buy: Ceramics are available at local artisan stores and marketplaces. Notable locations include:

Tavira Market: A weekly market where local craftsmen sell their handcrafted ceramics.
Casa das Artes: A boutique that promotes local art and crafts, often displaying ceramic pieces by local artisans.

2. Textile and Embroidery

Tavira has a long textile legacy, notably for its high-quality linens and finely embroidered items. The artistry used to create these fabrics reflects abilities handed down through generations.

Key features:

Embroidered Tablecloths and Napkins: Featuring elaborate motifs, these products are ideal for bringing a bit of Portuguese flair to your house.
Traditional Clothing: Handcrafted clothes like capes and shawls are also available, highlighting indigenous patterns and skills.

Where To Buy:

Local Artisan Shops: Many tiny businesses in Tavira sell embroidered textiles.

Local craft fairs provide an opportunity to acquire unique handcrafted things directly from craftspeople.

3. Handcrafted Jewelry

The Algarve is noted for its exquisite jewelry, which often incorporates locally available materials like cork, ceramics, and silver. Artisans make one-of-a-kind items that capture the region's natural splendor.

Key features:

Cork Jewelry: Portugal is the world's biggest supplier of cork, and many craftsmen make stunning jewelry items from this eco-friendly material.
Silver Jewelry: Traditional silver filigree methods are used to produce elaborate patterns, which are often influenced by nature.

Where To Buy:

Jewelry stores: Tavira has various stores that specialize in selling local jewelry, such as Joalharia Tavira, where you may discover unique handmade items.
Artisan marketplaces: Look for local marketplaces where jewelers showcase their work.

4. Cork Products

Cork is an important component of Portuguese culture and the economy, and Tavira is no exception. Cork products are flexible and environmentally beneficial, used in everything from fashion to home design.

Key features:

Tourists choose cork purses and wallets because they are stylish and lightweight.
Home Decor Items: Cork coasters, placemats, and ornamental items are excellent mementos.

Where To Buy:

Cork Shops: Tavira features specialist businesses that sell a range of cork items, including Cork & Co.
Local Craft Markets: Many craftsmen sell their cork creations at craft shows.

5. Art Prints and Paintings

Tavira's breathtaking surroundings and rich history have inspired several local painters. Buying art prints or original paintings is a great way to take a bit of Tavira home with you.

Key features:

Local Scenes: Many painters strive to capture the beauty of Tavira, its architecture, and the surrounding surroundings.

Various Mediums: There are a variety of art types available, including watercolor and oil paintings, as well as digital prints.

Where To Buy:

Art Galleries: For one-of-a-kind artworks, visit local galleries like Galeria Trem.

Artisan Markets: Many markets include local artists selling prints and paintings.

6. Traditional Honey with Olive Oil

Tavira is also famous for its exquisite local goods, notably honey and olive oil, which make great food keepsakes.

Key features:

Tavira honey is well-known for its rich taste and quality since it is often derived from local beekeepers.

Olive Oil: The area produces high-quality olive oil, which is available in nicely wrapped bottles.

Where To Buy:

Local businesses: Tavira has several businesses that specialize in local products, including honey and olive oil. Farmers' markets are where you may discover artisanal food producers selling their products.

7. Souvenirs with Stories

Many local crafts come with intriguing tales about their origins or cultural importance. When buying souvenirs, ask the craftsmen about their work to acquire a better understanding of the objects you choose.

Tips for Shopping in Tavira

Bargaining: In marketplaces, some bargaining may be okay, particularly if you're buying many products.
Cash: While most establishments take credit cards, smaller artisan stores may prefer cash, so have some euros on hand.

Support Local craftspeople: Whenever feasible, purchase directly from craftspeople. This guarantees that your money benefits the local economy and preserves traditional crafts.

Popular Shopping Centers in Tavira

1. Tavira Market

Tavira Market, commonly known as Mercado da Ribeira, is a must-see for everyone who wants to experience local life. This lively market takes place every Saturday and is situated in the town center. It's a fantastic place to buy fresh food, local specialties, and handcrafted items.

What To Expect:

Local Produce: Fresh fruits, vegetables, and herbs grown on local farms.
Artisanal Products: A wide range of handcrafted objects, such as textiles, pottery, and jewelry, which are often sold directly by the craftspeople.
Food Stalls: Try some local delights including cured meats, cheeses, and pastries.

2. Tavira Shopping Center

Tavira Shopping, located just outside the town center, is the area's primary shopping center, including a variety of retail stores, restaurants, and entertainment choices. It provides a more contemporary shopping experience than the conventional market.

What To Expect:

Brand Stores: A variety of national and international brands, such as apparel, gadgets, and cosmetics.

Restaurants and cafés: Where you may get a bite to eat or have a coffee break after shopping.

Entertainment: A theater showcasing the most recent films, making it ideal for families and groups.

3. Corte Inglés de Faro

While not in Tavira, the Corte Inglés department store in Faro is only a short drive away and one of the Algarve's biggest and most popular shopping destinations.

What To Expect:

Corte Inglés offers a wide range of products, including apparel, accessories, gadgets, and gourmet cuisine.

Luxury labels: With a collection of high-end fashion labels, it is a popular choice among luxury buyers.

Gourmet Food Section: An amazing food hall with local and worldwide delicacies, ideal for purchasing gourmet presents.

If you want a more extensive shopping experience or specialized luxury products, a visit to Corte Inglés is worthwhile. It's also an excellent location for finding one-of-a-kind items to bring home.

4. Tavira Shopping Center

This retail complex, situated in the town center, is well-known for its small boutiques and specialized stores. It's a great location to discover local clothes and crafts.

What To Expect:

Local boutiques provide one-of-a-kind apparel, accessories, and artisan goods that cannot be bought in bigger retailers.
Cafés & bistros: There are many eating alternatives where you may get a meal or a coffee while shopping.

5. Liberdade Street

Rua do Liberdade is one of Tavira's principal shopping alleys, lined with a wide range of stores, from traditional crafts to sophisticated boutiques.

What To Expect:

Artisan Shops: There are several boutiques that sell handcrafted products such as pottery, textiles, and jewelry.
Local Restaurants: There are several eating alternatives available, enabling you to take a break from shopping and sample local food.

6. Olhao Fish Market

The Olhao Fish Market, located only a short drive from Tavira, offers a one-of-a-kind shopping experience, particularly for seafood aficionados. This crowded market is one of the greatest locations to purchase fresh seafood from the Atlantic.

What To Expect:

Fresh Seafood: A wide selection of fish, shellfish, and other seafood items available for purchase.
Local sellers: Talk to local fishermen and sellers who sell their daily catch.

7. Artisan Workshops and Studios

Tavira is home to various artisan workshops where tourists may buy handcrafted things straight from the creators. These classes often concentrate on traditional crafts including ceramics, textiles, and woodworking.

What To Expect:

Hands-on Experience: Some workshops allow you to engage in crafting sessions, which makes it a memorable experience.

Unique Souvenirs: Items acquired directly from artists can have a narrative or personal touch.

8. Antique and Vintage Shops

Tavira features various antique and vintage stores that sell a variety of antiquities and oddities.

What To Expect:

Antique Furniture and décor: A diverse selection of products, including old furniture, décor, and collectibles.
Local Memorabilia: One-of-a-kind objects that tell Tavira's narrative and history.

Tavira provides a fascinating shopping experience that combines contemporary retail with traditional crafts. There is something for everyone, whether you want to explore local markets, go shopping, or find artisan crafts. Tavira's retail sector represents the Algarve region's rich culture and creativity, with fresh produce, handcrafted crafts, unique souvenirs, and gourmet meals.

Chapter 8

Nightlife Activities in Tavira

T avira is well-known for its beautiful beaches, rich history, and exquisite architecture. However, as the sun goes down, Tavira comes alive with a range of nightlife activities for residents and visitors. Tavira has a wide choice of nocturnal activities, from busy pubs and clubs to peaceful riverfront walks and cultural concerts. Here's a comprehensive look at the nightlife options in Tavira.

1. Bars and Lounges

Tavira has a variety of pleasant pubs and lounges where you can relax with friends or meet new ones. The ambiance at these establishments often combines historic Portuguese charm with a contemporary flair.

Café del Mar Tavira: This popular location is noted for its laid-back atmosphere and breathtaking river views. Enjoy a beverage or a bottle of local wine while viewing the sunset.

Dona Ana: Located near the Tavira marina, Dona Ana has a lively ambiance with live music on some evenings. It's a great spot for tapas and beverages.

Tavira Lounge: A trendy bar with a variety of beverages and a nice atmosphere ideal for mingling. The pub periodically organizes DJ nights, making it an ideal location for people seeking to dance.

2. Live Music and Cultural Events

Tavira's nightlife is supplemented by its cultural attractions, with a variety of venues featuring live music performances and cultural events all year.

Cultural Events at the Tavira Cultural Center: This facility often hosts concerts by local musicians, theatrical groups, and art exhibits. Keep an eye on their calendar for future events featuring local talent.

Jazz and Blues evenings: Some Tavira clubs, such as the Tavira Jazz Club, have themed music evenings, which provide a fantastic chance to see live performances by local and visiting musicians.

3. Dining Experiences

Tavira's nightlife relies mostly on eating out. The area is home to various restaurants that provide delectable gastronomic experiences, sometimes accompanied by a lively ambiance.

Restaurante O Castelo: Located in the center of Tavira, this restaurant provides classic Portuguese cuisine. The outside dining area is ideal for a relaxing evening dinner, particularly in warm weather.

Casa da Caldeirada: This restaurant is known for its seafood delicacies and has a quiet setting, making it perfect for a relaxing meal after a day of exploring.

4. Riverside Strolls

Tavira's position along the Gilão River offers a magnificent setting for relaxing evening strolls. The riverfront is dotted with palm trees and lovely paths, making it ideal for a romantic stroll or a relaxing evening.

Tavira Waterfront: The area along the river is brilliantly lighted at night, providing a peaceful environment. Stop at one of the numerous benches to take in the scenery or relax.

The landmark pedestrian bridge provides a beautiful perspective of the river and town at night. Walking over it may be a delightful experience, particularly with the reflection of lights on the lake.

5. Clubs and Dance Venues

Tavira has a few clubs and late-night places where you can catch DJ sets and dance music.

Mikasa Club: Located just outside Tavira, this club plays a variety of music types, including techno and pop. It targets a younger demographic and often has themed parties and events.

Kasa do Povo: A popular local hangout, this club is noted for its energetic atmosphere and periodically offers dance nights with local DJs.

6. Wine and Port Tasting

Tavira's closeness to various vineyards makes it ideal for wine and port tastings. Many area vineyards provide nighttime tours and tastings, enabling visitors to experience the region's tastes.

Quinta da Rocha: This vineyard provides guided tours, followed by samples of their wines and ports, allowing you to learn about the local winemaking process.

Algarve Wine Tours: Some businesses provide evening wine tours that take you to different vineyards where you may drink local wines while admiring the picturesque surroundings.

7. Festivals and fairs

Tavira features a variety of events and fairs throughout the year, which contribute to the city's nightlife. These gatherings often include live music, local food, and cultural acts.

Tavira Carnival: This vivid event, usually held in February, features parades, music, and dancing, converting the town into a joyous environment.
Feira de Artesanato: This crafts fair, which frequently takes place during the summer months, features local artists and allows visitors to purchase unique handcrafted things while listening to live music.

8. Game Nights and Trivia

Consider attending local pub and bar game nights or trivia contests for a more casual evening. These activities may be a great opportunity to meet new people and connect with the local community.

Tavira Sports pub: Known for its warm ambiance, this pub sometimes holds trivia nights and games, making it an ideal location for friendly competition.

Community activities: Keep a watch on local bulletin boards and social media sites for information about game nights and activities hosted by the community.

9. Cultural and Historical Tours

Exploring Tavira's history and culture does not have to end at dusk. Several businesses provide nocturnal tours of the town, giving visitors a fresh viewpoint on its historical attractions.

Nighttime Ghost Tours: Some local guides provide eerie tours of Tavira, including ghost tales and folklore about the town's past, which is ideal for people interested in the supernatural.

Cultural Walks: Join guided walks that highlight Tavira's history, architecture, and cultural importance, enabling you to learn more about the town while enjoying the lower evening weather.

Tavira's nightlife is a beautiful combination of calm and lively activities, appealing to a wide range of interests and inclinations.

Chapter 9

Itinerary Plan for Tourists

A 14-day itinerary for Tavira, a charming town enables tourists to see its rich culture, breathtaking scenery, and adjacent attractions. This plan balances the steady exploration of Tavira with day trips to adjacent cities, beaches, and natural parks, resulting in a well-rounded experience.

Day 1: Arrive in Tavira

Accommodation Check-in: Arrive and settle into your hotel or rental.

Explore Tavira Town: Take a stroll through the gorgeous streets, see the Roman Bridge, and admire the beautiful architecture.

Dinner: Restaurante O Castelo serves authentic Algarve food.

Day 2: Discover Tavira.

Tavira Castle: Visit the remains and enjoy panoramic views of the town.

Cultural Exploration: Go to the Tavira Museum to learn about local history.

Lunch: Have lunch at a nearby café, such as Café del Mar.

Riverside stroll: Enjoy an evening stroll along the Gilão River.

Day 3: Beach Day at Praia do Barril.

Morning: Take a quick rail journey or stroll to Praia do Barril.

Activities include relaxing on the beach, swimming, and trying watersports such as paddleboarding.

Lunch: Have a seaside dinner at one of the eateries.

Afternoon: Visit the Anchorage Museum and the remarkable Anchors Cemetery.

Day 4: Trip to Faro.

Morning: Travel to Faro by bus (approximately 30 minutes).

Explore Faro: See the Old Town, Carmo Church, and Faro Municipal Museum.

Lunch: Visit Faro's Mercado do 2 de Maio and try local specialties.

Evening: return to Tavira for supper.

Day 5: Visit Cacela Velha.

Morning: Travel to Cacela Velha (approximately 15 minutes by vehicle or bus).

Visit the stunning Cacela Velha Castle for spectacular vistas.

Relax in Praia da Fábrica.

Dinner: Visit Onda Norte, which is noted for its delicious seafood.

Day 6: Outdoor Adventure at Ria Formosa Natural Park

Morning: Take a guided trip or hire a kayak to explore Ria Formosa.

Birdwatching: See a variety of bird species, including flamingos and herons.

Picnic picnic: Bring a picnic to eat in the park.

Evening: Return to Tavira for a relaxing meal.

Day 7: Visit Olhão.

Morning: Take a bus to Olhão (approximately 20 minutes).

Explore Olhão by visiting the fish market and walking through the lovely streets.

Lunch: Visit a local restaurant and eat seafood.

Beach Time: Spend the day on Ilha da Culatra, a neighboring island accessible by boat.

Day 8: Leisure Day in Tavira.

Spa Day: Schedule a spa treatment at your hotel or a nearby facility.

Explore the local stores for souvenirs and crafts.

Lunch: Take a leisurely lunch at Casa da Caldeirada.

Evening: If possible, attend a local musical or cultural event.

Day 9: Day trip to Lagos.

Morning: Travel to Lagos (approximately an hour by rail).

Explore Lagos: Visit Ponta da Piedade for breathtaking seaside vistas.

Lunch: Eat at Restaurante dos Artistas.

Evening: Return to Tavira for a leisurely meal.

Day 10: Wine tasting tour.

Morning: Take a guided wine tour in the Algarve area.

Lunch: Have dinner at one of the vineyards.

Evening: Return to Tavira for supper at a nearby restaurant.

Day 11: Discover Tavira's beaches.

Beach Hopping: Spend the day exploring other beaches, such as Praia de Tavira and Praia do Homem Nu.

Activities include swimming, sunbathing, and visiting coastal bars.

Lunch: Have a picnic on the beach.

Evening: Dine at Pé na Água, a popular place with sea views.

Day 12: Visit Silves.

Morning: Make a day excursion to Silves (approximately one hour by bus).

Explore Silves: See the beautiful Silves Castle and Silves Cathedral.

Lunch: Restaurante Café Inglês serves classic Portuguese cuisine.

Evening: return to Tavira for supper.

Day 13: Adventure in the Monchique Mountains.

Morning: Travel to Monchique (approximately an hour by driving).

Hiking: Explore the routes in the Monchique Mountains and appreciate the breathtaking vistas.

Lunch: Eat in a mountain restaurant, such as Restaurante O Luar da Fóia.

Evening: return to Tavira for a goodbye meal.

Day 14: Departure.

Last-Minute Shopping: Spend your last morning shopping for keepsakes.

Relax: Have a leisurely breakfast at your lodgings. Departure: Check out and transfer to the airport or your next destination.

General Tips for the 14-Day Itinerary:

- Transportation: To effectively travel the Algarve area, use local buses or trains.
- Local Cuisine: Sample traditional foods such as cataplana, piri-piri chicken, and local fish.
- Stay Hydrated: The Algarve can be rather warm, particularly in the summer; always bring water with you when you go out.
- Flexible Planning: Allow for flexibility in your plan; you can find new favorite places!

Common Tourist Mistakes to Avoid

When visiting a new place, such as Tavira, travelers often make basic blunders that detract from their experience. Here are examples of these mistakes, along with advice on how to prevent them:

1. Underestimating travel time.

Many people underestimate the amount of time it takes to go from one location to another, particularly in an area with picturesque but twisting roads. To prevent this, plan your route with realistic travel times and allow time for unanticipated delays.

2. Not Learning Basic Local Language Phrases.

While many residents in Tavira understand English, learning a few basic Portuguese words helps improve relationships and demonstrate respect for the local culture. Simple statements like "Obrigado" (Thank you) and "Por favor" (Please) may have a significant impact.

3. Ignoring Local Customs and Etiquette.
Understanding and honoring local traditions is critical. For example, in Portugal, it is common to welcome with a handshake and the words "Bom dia" (Good morning) or

"Boa tarde" (Good afternoon). Familiarize oneself with these conventions to prevent unintended mistakes.

4. Not trying local cuisine.

Some travelers choose to eat familiar meals rather than sample local cuisine. Tavira has superb seafood and authentic Algarve cuisine that tourists should not miss. Consider sampling some local favorites, such as cataplana or piri-piri chicken.

5. Rushing through attractions

Travelers sometimes attempt to pack too many events into a single day, which leads to exhaustion. Instead, focus on a few essential attractions and make time to experience each one. Tavira's attractiveness stems from its sluggish pace.

6. Failing to book accommodations in advance

During busy seasons, rooms tend to fill up rapidly. To minimize last-minute stress and increased expenses, book your stay ahead of time, particularly if you intend to come during the summer.

7. Overpacking

Tourists often pack too much stuff, making travel difficult. Pack lightly and include adaptable attire ideal for a variety of activities, as well as comfortable walking shoes.

8. Failure to check weather conditions

Tavira's weather might change, and forgetting to check the forecast may cause discomfort. Make sure to prepare appropriately, packing clothes for chilly nights and sun protection for day trips.

9. Ignoring transportation options.

Some travelers depend only on taxis or rental automobiles, ignoring the fact that public transportation is often more convenient and cost-effective. Look for local buses or trains that may transport you to nearby attractions.

10. Not Engaging with Locals

Tourists often miss out on the finest experiences by sticking to popular tourist destinations. Engage with locals to get tips for hidden treasures like lesser-known eateries or off-the-beaten-path activities.

Conclusion

Travelers may make the most of their stay in Tavira by avoiding these typical blunders. For further information on traveling and making the most of your vacation, consult resources from travel specialists or local tourist boards.

SAFE TRAVEL

Printed in Great Britain
by Amazon